MAXIMUM WEIGHT LOSS,
MINIMUM EFFORT

A guide to losing weight for people who love food -

and hate exercise!

ANTHONY WILLIAMS

CONTENTS

PREFACE TO THE NEW EDITION

I'm going to start by saying something you may find it surprizing for an author to say.

You might not like this book. You might even hate it.

Why do I say this? Well, here's the thing. In the two or so years since I first published this short book, I've occasionally checked the reviews. Not necessarily to massage my ego (although I'd be lying if I said there wasn't an element of that!). But more because I am genuinely interested in what people have to say about it. I honestly want to know if it's helping people or not.

What I've found is that it's a bit like Marmite in that people either seem to love it or hate it. The people that love it have used words such as 'inspiring', 'straight forward', 'direct', 'relatable', 'makes sense'. The ones that hate it use words such as 'disappointing', 're-dundant', 'not worth buying'.

Interestingly, alot of the time, the same words are used by both camps. For example, both people that love it *and* people that hate it comment on the length of the book (it's definitely not War & Peace). Some love the fact that they can read it in one sitting, others seem to be disappointed that it's not a lengthier tome with tonnes of words, details, lists and figures.

I suppose the one thing that strikes me about the reviews that are negative is that the authors of them were perhaps expecting something else, so in that respect perhaps I owe them an apology. I'll make it clear now: this isn't the type of book that is full of scientific research, strictly calculated eating plans, and the kind of detail that you can pore over for weeks and weeks. In fact I deliberately avoided writing the book in this way, for the simple reason that my own weight loss journey was based on very simple and practical ideas which may initially seem 'redundant' (as one reviewer called them), but which, in fact, worked very effectively for me. And as such there's no reason why they couldn't work for others who wish to lose some of their excess weight.

It saddens me somewhat that the people who hated the book were prepared to write it off without actually indicating that they had tried to follow the steps I outline in it. If they had done so and failed to lose weight, then fair enough! But the general theme of the bad reviews seems to be 'it's too short and simple, therefore it can't possibly work and I hate it'.

So, as I say at the beginning, you too might hate this little book. But equally, you might love it and find it a useful and inspiring resource for weight loss, as many others have. I suppose there's only one way to find out - by reading it!

INTRODUCTION

There are countless books about how to lose weight, infinite diets which have been dreamt up, innumerable experts telling people what they should do to shift the pounds. There are all sorts of weight loss remedies available in the shops and online, promising a quick and easy solution to losing weight. And you can find any number of nutritionists and personal trainers who'll charge you a small fortune to stick to gruelling, depressing regimes.

But how many of these (no doubt well-meaning) ideas and initiatives have really had any success in helping people lose their excess weight, and more importantly, keep it off? Well personally, I don't know. And I don't really care. Because I found a way to lose weight without the help of any of the things mentioned above.

I always had an image of myself as a slim person, which I had been for most of my life. When I started seeing photos of myself with a double chin and a protruding belly, initially I tried to laugh them off as simply being taken at an unflattering angle; after all I didn't look like that in real life. Did I? Well yes, I did. I've decided to included my 'before and after' pictures so you can see for yourself:

When I faced up to the fact that that my weight had crept up to a point where I was technically classed as overweight, and two stone (28lbs / 12.7kgs) above where I had been for most of my adult life, I decided to do something about it.

Now I don't know about you, but I'm quite lazy. I've always been a bit stubborn and resistant to doing something just because others tell me to. I'm not a huge fan of exercise, having never been inside a gym in my life. And I can't stand the thought of sticking to some faddy, taste-free diet for the rest of my life, avoiding all the foods that I actually enjoy – I'd actually rather be overweight! Substitute tasty daily meals for some horrid health-drink? No thanks! Sign up to some weight-loss group where I have to talk about my weight with a bunch of strangers? Sounds like absolute hell to me!

Taking all this into account, I knew that there was no point going down the route of an established diet plan thought out by some weight-obsessed health guru, maybe combined with a dreaded exercise regime which I wouldn't have a hope in hell of sticking to. No, I was going to do this my way or no way. So what did I do, you ask? Well, I started thinking about food. Because thinking is surely a good place to start! I'd still eat what I wanted, when I wanted. I'd just give a bit more thought to what I was actually eating. And lo and behold, I saw some pretty amazing results!

Sounds too good to be true, right? Well, maybe. I'm not saying I've come up with some miracle weight loss plan which is fool-proof and guaranteed. I'm not saying you'll find my ideas so easy you could follow them in your sleep. All I know for sure is that, to my quiet surprise, my plan worked. Within 4 months of deciding to lose weight, I had lost two stone and was back to the weight I'd been in my 20's (having just reached my early 40's). And when I thought about how good I felt about this, and how relatively easy I'd found it, especially knowing how much some people struggle with losing weight, I just thought maybe I could share my ideas with other people. After all, why keep them a secret?

In these five simple, easy to read chapters, I share the story of how I managed to lose weight without losing my mind, cutting out my favorite foods or turning into a gym bunny!

I'm not a scientist, or a doctor. I'm not a weight-loss expert. I don't have any qualifications in this field, nor do I claim to. I'm just a regular person who was uncomfortable with his weight and decided to do something about it. And I seem to have hit on something which worked for me. And if it can work for food-loving, gym-avoiding, rule-dodging old me, well just maybe it could work for you too...

CHAPTER 1 – THINK!

I truly believe that the most important thing you can do to lose weight is to think about food. This may sound a bit odd, but let me explain.

My weight loss started in my mind. I decided to lose weight, and once the mental seed was planted, it's something I vowed to keep hold of and nurture as much as possible. I hatched a plan to think about food more. Not eat it more, just think about it more. Not OBSSESS about it, just think about it, regularly. Easy, right? Well, yes and no.

We all eat several times a day. But how often do we actually THINK about what we're eating? Ever found yourself sitting in front of the TV polishing off a whole chocolate bar or large bag of potato chips? Going out for a meal and deciding before you've even finished the first mouthful that you will be clearing your plate of this delicious food, regardless of whether you start feeling full or the restaurant starts burning down? Of course you have – we all have! All well and good – life's hard enough, and food is one of the few things we can rely on to make us feel happy. You worked hard to afford that food on your plate, and you deserve to enjoy it – so enjoy it!

But just take a moment to think. You KNOW that overeating (that is, eating beyond the point of feeling full) isn't healthy. You just choose to IGNORE that knowledge. Whilst eating, you choose to distract yourself by watching TV, or checking your phone, or chatting to your partner as you munch away. So we stop thinking as we're eating; the connection between food and mind is blocked or even severed entirely.

Well, here's an idea; just THINK! Before you buy the food, think about it. Think about what's in it, think about what else you've eaten today, what else you're planning to eat later. There's no need to judge yourself, or deny yourself that meal you've been looking forward to, or that treat you suddenly fancy. Just get a mental picture of the food and focus on it for a moment or two.

As you're eating your food, THINK about the fact that you're eating, and what it is that you're eating. Enjoying that chocolate, or those chips? That sumptuous meal in your favorite restaurant? Fantastic – all power to you.

But just THINK as you're eating. BE AWARE that you're eating. And ENJOY what you're eating! Really enjoy the aromas, taste the flavours, notice the textures. Feel the sensation of the food in your mouth. Chew it to extract the maximum enjoyment, and notice it as it slips down your gullet and into your stomach. Take your time. Think. It may help to switch off or turn down the TV. Maybe put your phone down and leave Facebook scrolling until afterwards. Quit worrying about that issue you had at work today. Focus on the here and now, the food you are eating – this is your primary concern for the next few minutes.

So why am I suggesting that you think about food if you're just going to go ahead and eat it anyway? After all, it's not like you can just magically wish away the calories, is it!

Well, the idea behind the concept of THINKING about your food is to help you forge a new, meaningful relationship with it. Sometimes we get into habits so easily that we do things without even thinking. Take breathing for example – we don't think about it, we just do it. Food is a bit like this – it's something we need to survive, but we sometimes consume it with barely any thought at all. And because this is the trap we've fallen into at some point, we somehow feel there's no way out of it, or no alternative. But this is very far from the truth.

'Mindfulness' is a word which is bandied around quite a lot these days, usually relating to meditation or mental health matters. But it can also be applied to your PHYSICAL health in relation to what you are putting in your body. By THINKING about what we eat, we re-establish the link between the mind and the stomach. And if we get into the habit of doing this every single time we eat, we'll really start to pay more attention to the bad habits we've developed – the snacking, the overeating, the eating out of boredom rather than hunger. And when we become conscious of these habits, and recognize that they are unhelpful, our mind will set itself on a path to reduce these habits and eventually avoid them altogether.

The mind is a very powerful thing. I'm going to make you try a little exercise here – but don't worry, it's a purely mental exercise! Imagine a large field of corn – beautiful, tall, dense corn, gently swaying in the wind. Imagine that this field of corn is on your journey to work, and you need to make your way through it in order to reach your destination. So one day you beat a path through this lovely corn, stamping and flattening it in front of you with your feet as you make your way across this field. However, when you get to the end of the field there's a giant, scary, slathering dog, barking aggressively at you. You have to run like mad to get away from this crazy dog so it doesn't bite you. Well, the next day when you go to work, you get to the field and find that the flat pathway through the field that you made yesterday is still there, therefore the easiest way to get across the cornfield is to take exactly the same path. It's literally 'the path of least resistance'. But once again, when you get to the end of the path there's the same nasty dog, desperate to take a chunk out of you. Same again the next day. Man, what an annoying dog, if only there was a way to avoid it!

On the fourth day you realise that you've had enough of this horrid hound, and you decide to start your journey at a different entry point in the field. So you beat a new path through the field. It's quite hard going (certainly harder than taking the path of nice flat corn that you'd made for yourself). But you're smart, and you've brought a plank of wood with you, which you place in front of you as you move forward, helping to flatten the corn. And when you get to the end of the field this time, emerging far away from the exit point that you used the last few days, you discover to your delight that there's no dog! Result!! So from now on you use this new path through the cornfield on your journey to work, and this new path now becomes your path of least resistance, whilst the corn on the other path that you made (leading to the dog) starts gradually springing back up again until there's no trace of the original path.

Well your mind is like the cornfield; it can be manipulated. Your weight gain is like the dog – it's an unpleasant but completely predictable result at the end of a well-trodden path. The plank of wood is like the guidance that I'm providing you with in this book, helping you make your new path across the field as smooth and painless as possible, and leading to a much happier outcome than your old path. Do you follow? I hope so!

There is actually some science behind what I'm saying. If you don't believe me, Google 'neuroplasticity' and see what you find.

It's not easy, and it takes time. But just try it. Next time you eat, just THINK. When you have your breakfast tomorrow, THINK. Do the same at lunchtime, and at dinner, and any time you have a snack. THINK. And just by doing this, you'll already be taking the most important, most useful step towards weight loss that you could ever imagine.

CHAPTER 2 –DRINK!

This is an easy one. Want a quick, simple way to make yourself feel fuller, reducing the amount you eat and therefore helping you lose weight? Well, have a drink. A big one. Every time you eat something.

Liquid is often thought of as the less important element of our diet. It's not quite as exciting as food, is it? Well, unless it contains alcohol, but that brings its own problems with it!

But it's really important to get in the habit of drinking. Any dietician or health guru will tell you about the importance of hydration. But we shouldn't make the mistake of just having a drink when we feel thirsty – by that point we're already drying out! Instead, make a point of having a drink at each mealtime.

So what should you drink? Well, I'd suggest having a good-sized glass of orange juice or other fruit juice with your breakfast, and a pint of water or squash with your lunch, and the same again with your dinner. Have a third of the drink before you start to eat, a third as you're eating your meal, and a third at the end of your meal. Don't wait until you've finished your food – if you do this, you risk filling your stomach up too much with solid sustenance, leaving no room for the liquid.

During the day, keep a bottle of water on your desk (or in your work vehicle) and sip from this regularly. Oh, and try to limit the alcohol and fizzy drinks, both of which have an awful lot of calories and will de-hydrate you.

Personally, I love carbonated water and have come to view it as something of a treat. A fizzy drink with no calories, no additives (other than bubbles) and total hydration? Bring it on!

This was a very easy chapter to write, and it's a very, very easy one to put into practice.

So the two simple steps so far are THINK and DRINK! Got them? Great, here's the next one!

CHAPTER 3 – LISTEN!

I've found that by LISTENING to your internal voice you'll quickly learn to tune into the messages which everyone has the ability to receive from their own bodies and minds, but so few of us actually choose to acknowledge, let alone act on. In relation to food, these messages come from two different areas: the mind and the stomach.

First off, your mind.

As you THINK and find your mind tuning in to what you are eating, notice how you suddenly start hearing a little voice in the back of the mind which says things like this:

'Too much of this is bad for you'.

'You already had something unhealthy earlier today, maybe you should stick to healthy stuff for the rest of the day'.

'You're actually not hungry at all, why are you eating?'.

Now, this voice might be irritating to you. You might even visualize the words as though they are being spoken by the person in this world who you dislike the most. Your natural reaction might be to ignore the voice or tell it to shut up. But the thing is, as much as you may hate it, the voice is RIGHT.

Your parents undoubtedly tried to teach you right from wrong. Other influences in your life – teachers, relatives, friends – would have reinforced these teachings as you grew up. For example, if you trespass on railway lines, you're at risk of electrocution. If you drive recklessly, you risk injuring yourself (or others). These thoughts are so ingrained in your mind that they become an integral part of it. Most of the time they sit there without you noticing them, but every now and then, when the circumstances arise, they float to the surface of your mind and manifest in the form of an internal voice.

Let's say you're in a position of authority at work, and have access to the company bank account or check book. You're a little short of money this month, and you work for a big company which is trading very profitably. Why not access the company bank account and transfer a little bit extra into your own personal bank account, or write yourself a juicy check to tide you over? Well, there's a good reason why, and it's totally separate from the moral argument. You know full well that if you get caught (as there's a good chance you eventually will), you'll end up in big trouble. You'll almost certainly lose your job. You could even end up in prison. Ultimately, you want to avoid the wrongful action not because it's *morally* wrong, but because it has the very real potential to cause you significant unhappiness and hardship. In other words, you're protecting YOURSELF.

As a result of the experiences you've had and the lessons you've learned along life's way, when you're presented with a situation like the one above, a little voice in your mind inevitably pipes up, saying 'NO, you mustn't do that! It won't help you. It will ultimately make you unhappy. Just don't'. And you listen to this voice (well, hopefully you do!). Because you know the voice is CORRECT in what it's saying (even if you picture the voice coming out of that stupid guy in the office that you can't stand!).

Well, it's this same voice which talks to you about food. But because this is 'only' food we're talking about (not a spell in prison), it's not so important to listen to this voice. In fact, to hell with it! Right? WRONG. Now's the time to start listening. The voice is talking sense. It wants to help you protect yourself. So LISTEN to it!

So that's the mind sorted, but how on earth do you listen to your stomach, I hear you ask!

Imagine the scene; you're in a restaurant. You've ordered your favorite dish. It arrives, and it's delicious. You tuck in heartily. But hang on, what's this? You're maybe a third or a half of the way through this yummy meal, and suddenly you feel a little twinge in your stomach, almost as though it was saying it was full. How odd! Why would it say such a thing? Well the answer is – BECAUSE IT'S TRUE!

Unfortunately, we're so used to ignoring this voice that we simply plough on with clearing our plate. But how many times have you done this and then regretted this? Said to yourself 'I wish I'd stopped eating when I started to feel full'? When you think about it, isn't it completely nonsensical to do something you enjoy to such an extreme that it moves from being a source of pleasure to a source of pain and discomfort? The eyes really are bigger than the stomach, it seems. The trouble is, the stomach is a bit like a piece of elastic. It stretches. And if you keep on stretching it, it gets out of shape.

Well the good news is, it's really easy to overcome this little problem, and, unlike a stretched piece of elastic, you can reduce the size of your stomach pretty easily. Next time you feel that twinge in your stomach as you're part way through a meal, recognize it for what it is. It's your stomach talking to you, telling you it's full.

LISTEN to it. Put your knife and fork down, finish off your drink (remember chapter 2!), and stop. I promise you, you'll be so glad you stopped when you did.

You might think, 'oh but I'm paying for this food, surely I should eat it all?'. Or 'but my parents always taught me to clear my plate, so that's what I should do'. Don't let these thoughts drown out the messages which your own body and mind are giving you – after all, when you think about it logically these thoughts are complete nonsense. They are ridiculous excuses for overriding what your own body and mind are telling you loud and clear, if only you know how to LISTEN. And as you practice listening to your stomach, you'll start to find that you're eating less and less. Why? Because your stomach is now shrinking in front of your very eyes!! And every time it tells you it's full and you listen to it, it will shrink a tiny bit more. Great, huh?!

Your internal voice, whether the one in your mind or the one in your stomach, isn't there just to get on your nerves; believe it or not it's trying to help you. So LISTEN to it, hear what it's got to say, and make friends with it. Imagine a kind person who tries to give you good advice purely out of their care and concern for you. You'd think they were a good friend, wouldn't you? They may have a bit of an annoying voice, or you may not like what they have to say. But what's the sense in ignoring what they're trying to tell you? Your internal voice is like a good friend. LISTEN to it, and take its advice.

Remember, just THINK, DRINK and LISTEN. Not too difficult, is it? As you work on making these three simple concepts part of your everyday life in terms of your relationship with food, you've already learnt some really important tools to help you lose your excess weight. In fact, you've already learnt most of what you need to know. Told you it was easy, didn't I!

CHAPTER 4: WATCH!

The THINK, DRINK and LISTEN concepts of the first three chapters have given you everything you need in order to lay the foundations of an effective and practical weight loss solution. Now it's time to build the bricks & mortar, so to speak! This is where you put words into action, theory into practice - and start to see results.

As I mentioned in the introduction, I'm not one for following strict regimes. But what I've found very helpful in my own weight loss plan is to have some guidelines – albeit loose ones. After all, you can't very well expect to lose weight if you just eat whatever the hell you want. You already know that you'll never lose weight on a diet of fried, fatty foods and sugary fizzy drinks. So you have to consider your food intake and WATCH what you eat, ensuring that you still get enough of everything you need in order to nourish your body.

Forgive me but I'm now going to use the C word. Calories are those dreaded things which seem to indicate both how tasty something is and how fat it's going to make you! I think it can be unhelpful to get too hung up on numbers. But there's a few numbers in relation to calories which I found helpful to bear in mind, and I think that using these as a loose frame of reference will help you with your daily eating plan.

The recommended daily calorie intake for a man is 2,500, and for a woman, 2,000. I read in an article that most meals are generally between 500 and 750 calories. 'Naughty' things such as a slice of cake are similar to a meal in terms of calorie count, i.e. 500 – 750 calories (certainly at the higher end of the scale if consumed with cream or ice cream). Fruit & vegetables, on the other hand, have low calorie counts, say 50 – 100 calories per item / serving (assuming not fried!). As far as my plan is concerned, these are all the numbers you need to know.

I'm a male of average build and height, doing little to no regular exercise (sorry, doctor!), so I decided for the purposes of my weight loss that I was going to aim for consuming around 1,250 calories a day. Maybe a few more, maybe a few less. I wasn't going to count the calories in everything I ate, mainly because I couldn't be bothered researching the exact calorie content of everything I put in my mouth. I would just make a reasonable estimate, and keep an eye on my rough daily tally, keeping it as close to my target calorie intake as I could.

It is of course important to have a balanced diet; aim for your five portions a day of fruit and vegetables and try to get a mixture of protein (e.g. meat, eggs, soya), carbohydrates (pasta, bread, rice), fiber (cereals, beans) and fats (olive oil, butter) each day. See, the good thing about this weight loss strategy is that you can eat all the things that you usually do, and not feel guilty about it!

So what rough calorie target should you set for yourself? Well, as obvious as it may sound, the lower you set your target, the more weight you will lose. HOWEVER, you want to ensure you are still getting adequate nourishment every day; if you simply cut the calories right down to the bone you're effectively going on a crash diet, and we know how unhelpful these are, right? So I'd suggest that you aim for somewhere between 1,000 and 1,500 calories per day. At this level of calorie intake, you are still getting enough nourishment for your body (and hopefully staving off hunger, particularly if you are choosing to load up on low-calorie food items such as fruit & vegetables rather than chocolate!), yet you are nicely below the level whereby your body will maintain (or increase) its existing weight. So even without much in the way of physical exercise, your body is burning up more calories than it is absorbing. The result? Guaranteed weight loss!!

Let me give you some examples of what I'd typically eat in a day under my weight loss plan, remembering that I decided to aim for around 1,250 calories a day.

For breakfast, I would have a couple of pieces of fruit and a cup of tea or coffee (I don't consider calories in tea, coffee or other drinks worth counting!). Or maybe a nice bowl of porridge oats – also pretty low in calories (you can jazz this up with blueberries, strawberries and/or a bit of honey). So let's say breakfast comes to 150 calories (average of 75g per fruit serving x 2). Leaving me a good few calories to use up in the rest of the day – great!!

Lunch? Simple, I might make a cheese sandwich (going easy on the cheese) with some relish and a bit of salad and cucumber. Or make a delicious homemade tomato soup with a bit of fresh, crusty bread. Maybe a fillet of oily fish (e.g. mackerel) with a nice bit of rocket salad on the side (adding some chopped red peppers or onions to add some extra flavour). Oh, and of course not forgetting the DRINK of Chapter 2 – a nice pint of fruit squash, remembering to drink a third before, a third during and a third after the food. Again – ignore any calories in the drink! For any of these lunch options, I would estimate a calorie count of around 500.

So it's over halfway through the day and I've used up less than half of the calories out of my daily target (650 calories out of a target of 1,250). Great, now I don't have to feel guilty about having a nice dinner! Perhaps a nice portion of shepherd's pie? As a vegetarian I would always use soya mince, which is a great source of protein, and lower in fat than meat. Or I might make a homemade curry with a small portion of rice (skipping the flavoured naan breads &

poppadoms as these push the calorie count skywards). Or maybe something from the freezer such as a soya escalope with fresh vegetables and a few french fries - the frozen variety are great, and much healthier than the ones from the takeaway! I'd try to load up on vegetables rather than the fries - there's far fewer calories in vegetables, and of course they're super-nutritious. I might have two different types, e.g. broccoli & carrot, peas & beans, just to add a bit of variety and leave a little less room on the plate for the fries.

Again, I'd re-emphasize that it's not worth getting too hung up on precise calorie counting. Just use reasonable estimates to calculate the approximate total calories of each meal, and make a mental note of this figure to help you work out your daily calorie intake (if you have a bad short term memory, maybe write it down on a piece of paper, or on your phone). Try to keep this as close as possible to your target, but DON'T worry too much if you're a bit under or over.

If you're eating out at a restaurant (which I highly encourage - provided you remain a little disciplined!), it can be even easier to assess your calorie intake as these days the calorie count is often displayed next to the menu choices. Have a look at the difference in calories counts between the different meals - you may be in for a surprize!

Imagine you've decided to go for a really high calorie meal, like a fried breakfast or a fish & chip supper. THAT'S OK!! ENJOY IT! But just remember to follow the procedure of THINK, DRINK, and LISTEN. What you'll start finding is that you don't eat all the food on your plate because you're now eating CONSCIOUSLY. So let's say you've estimated that the total meal in front you is a rather hefty 1,000 calories. But because your relationship with food is changing, whereas in the past you'd have polished off the whole lot without a second thought, now things are different. You're in tune with yourself. You know what you're doing, you have a plan, and you have a target. You're in control. And you're now LISTENING to your internal voice, ready to stop eating as soon as it tells you to - remember that you don't have to eat everything on your plate just because it's there! So you stop when you've eaten about two-thirds of the meal; that's around 650 calories, out of a possible 1,000.

Now let's say on that same day you had a breakfast of 150 calories, and a lunch of 500. Total calorie count for today is 150 + 500 + 650 = 1,300 (maybe there were a few extra calories here & there – so what!). That's really not bad at all, and in fact it's well below the normal recommended calorie count for both men and women. That means you're on the way to losing weight. So give yourself a pat on the back – you're doing great!

Similarly, let's say you had a bit of a heavy lunch (maybe that pub lunch offer was just too inviting to resist), or treated yourself to small dessert, and you work out that you've used up around 1,000 calories by the middle of the day. No problem! Come dinner time, you'll probably be thinking, 'I should eat something now'. But your internal voice pipes up saying, 'Why? Just because this is the time you usually eat? You're not even hungry!'. And because you're learning to value and listen to your internal voice, you can say to yourself 'actually, you're right. I'm not going to force another meal down, adding to my calorie count unnecessarily. I'll wait to see if I feel hungry later; if so, I'll just have something light & healthy, a couple of carrot sticks, maybe an apple. Or maybe a small bowl of cereal with semi-skimmed milk. Thank you, internal voice!'.

One of the most important ways in which I learned to cut down my calorie intake for meals at home was to use a small plate at meal times, instead of the usual large dinner plate. This physically restricts the amount of food you can apportion yourself, forcing you to keep your calorie numbers lower than usual. You'd be surprised at how a small plate of food actually fills you up; again, if you're listening to the internal voices coming from your mind and your stomach, you'll recognize that a smaller plate of food is actually a far more appropriate portion than a gigantic dinner plate on which you can pile so much food that the amount on the plate far exceeds the capacity of your stomach. But because we're so accustomed to eating off large dinner plates, we just assume that they hold the 'right' amount of food for a meal, and so eat it all up, totally ignoring the messages our mind and our poor stomach are trying to tell us. But not any more!

Now I must put my hands up and admit something. I love eating out. I mean, I LOVE it! I'd do it every day if I could (and to be honest, I quite often do!). If you are going out for a meal, it's quite likely that you're consuming more calories than you would at home. Why? Well firstly, you're not in control of your portion size the way you are at home (especially now that you're using small plates to eat off).

But also, eating establishments are sneaky. They want you to spend as much money as possible. They don't really care about your calorie intake, and why would they? The more people eat, the richer the owners of the restaurant get!! So they encourage you to gorge yourself. 'Are you having a starter, sir?', 'would you like fries / any sides with that?', 'is that a small or a large?', 'can I show you the dessert menu?'. These are all questions you're likely to be asked if you're eating out, designed to make you shovel more and more calories down your throat.

Well guess what; you don't have to fall for their sneaky tricks. Be disciplined. 'No I wouldn't like a starter', 'no I don't want fries / sides with that', 'I'll have the small size please' (usually perfectly adequately sized anyway), 'no desserts for me thanks, I'm full up'. That's all you need to say. Don't line their pockets, and pay the price with not only your wallet but also your waistline. Just eat what you need to make yourself full - remember to LISTEN for your stomach's message - and then leave (or stick to DRINKS from then on). Get into this habit and you'll start seeing results – fast. And as a result, you don't have to feel guilty about eating out so often!

OK, so CALORIES are the first thing you need to WATCH. There's one other thing to WATCH – your progress!

If you're anything like me, once you've set your mind on losing weight you're hopping on and off the bathroom scales at any given opportunity, despairing when you see your weight has gone up, shrugging your shoulders when it's the same as last time, and doing a little dance when you see that you've lost a couple of pounds!

Well, to an extent this is OK – it's important to keep an eye on things to ensure you're on the right track. Just remember that weight loss is a bit like a car journey. It's rarely a straight line from A to B. Sometimes there'll be turnings which take you slightly off course or even back on yourself, in the opposite direction from where you intend to go. But the important thing is to carry on with the car journey until you reach your destination – otherwise you'd never get anywhere!

I'd recommend limiting yourself to weighing yourself every second day, just so you can monitor the little changes, whatever they may be. Again, don't get hung up on numbers! Just WATCH to see how you're doing so that you know you're on the right path.

By focusing on the THINK, DRINK & LISTEN strategy, you'll be cutting down your calorie intake from what your body was used to. It is a gradual process, as indeed it should be – crash diets are incredibly ineffective solutions to long-term weight loss, and can be dangerous. WATCH your weight, and aim to lose an average of two pounds (0.9kgs) per week; that's pretty steady progress, and it will all add up. If you find you're not quite achieving this, try reducing your estimated daily calorie count a little more; what could you start skipping or reducing just to get your daily count down a bit? Or alternatively, try increasing the amount of exercise you do. But bear in mind, I achieved my weight loss purely based on changing my perspective on food. I must admit that I do little to no regular meaningful exercise (which I know isn't ideal from a health point of view). My weight loss strategy is therefore based on doing exactly the same amount of exercise as you currently do, whether that's hitting the gym five times a week, or (like me), next to nothing.

You'll probably find (as I did) that the weight loss is most noticeable in the first few weeks, after which it begins to slow down (although still head in the right direction, overall). This is because initially the body is given a bit of a wake-up call – suddenly it's not getting the same number of calories it was used to, and it goes into a bit of a panic, shedding weight quite rapidly. As your body starts to adapt to your new food regime, it gets more comfortable with the reduced calorie intake, and therefore weight loss continues at a slower pace. But this is a sign that it's working, so don't be disheartened if you 'only' lose two pounds (0.9kgs) one week after losing four (1.8kgs) the week before, or even if the scales show that you've put on a pound or two on any given day! All that matters is: your average weight is reducing, and you are becoming healthier as a result.

With the strategies outlined in this book, you'll still be eating a nutritious, balanced and TASTY diet. You'll still allow yourself treats. You'll still go out for meals. You won't actually be denying yourself anything at all! The only difference is that now you are THINKING about your food, you are DRINKING plenty of liquid alongside your food, you are LISTENING to your internal voice when it sends you messages about food, and you are WATCHING your calorie count.

Following this plan, you WILL lose weight! And when you start to see how the weight is beginning to drop off (dance away in that bathroom!), you'll feel good and want to continue because you know it's working; you'll be excited to see how much more pro-gress you can make towards reaching your target weight. You'll be your own source of inspiration, driving yourself on to get better and better results.

In short, you'll be a whole new person - and of course, a slimmer one!

CHAPTER 5: ENJOY!

The one thing I've learned is that if you make weight loss a chore, you're more likely to fail. Completely cutting out foods you like, or trying to stick to a gruelling gym regime you know you ultimately can't keep up, will only make you unhappy, which in turn will probably lead you back to your old, unhealthy eating habits.

Remember that you've set yourself a challenge, you've armed yourself with the tools to achieve what you want to achieve. So ENJOY your journey, and have a little fun along the way!

One of the best ways you can learn to enjoy yourself whilst undertaking this weight loss programme is to allow yourself a cheat day. Maybe one day a week. Don't go crazy and shovel as much food into your stomach as you can – this will undo a lot of your hard work. But say you're out having coffee with a friend and fancy a bit of cake – have it, and don't feel guilty. You've EARNED that bit of cake, dammit! Of course, you may want to think about stopping eating the cake if you notice that it's filling you up (remember to LISTEN to your internal voice), but if you're really enjoying it, what the hell, eat it all and lick the plate clean if you want! You've got another 6 days this week when you're going to be a little bit more careful, so one day out of seven is really no big deal.

Similarly, if you are on holiday, cut yourself a little slack - it's fine to have the cooked breakfast every day, if that's what takes your fancy! And maybe treat yourself to an occasional ice cream in the evening (what is it about ice cream that makes it taste so much nicer in a foreign country?!). Don't worry too much about weighing yourself while you're away; just make sure you get on the scales when you're back home so you can assess the 'damage' (and if you're anything like me, you'll find it almost impossible NOT to put weight on while on holiday!). Then consider where your target calorie count needs to be in order to get you back where you want to be weight-wise, and be a little more disciplined than you were on your hard-earned break.

Another way to continue to enjoy your weight loss journey is to eat whatever you want. Confused? Let me explain.

There's a very funny scene in the comedy sketch show 'Little Britain'. Marjorie Dawes, the sadistic and inept leader of a weight loss group ('Fat Fighters'), is giving her group attendees tips on losing weight. She tells them to take their favorite food (whatever this may be) and simply cut it in half, thereby halving the calories. 'And because it's half the calories, you can have twice as much!', she proclaims to the bemusement of her group.

Well actually, there is some wisdom in what Marjorie says, at least in the part before the punchline. What I've found is that you can – in fact you SHOULD – still eat your favorite foods. This could be chocolate, curry, potato chips, popcorn – it doesn't matter. The point is, in order to continue to get enjoyment out of food, you shouldn't feel that your favorite foods are off limits. So have them. BUT! The first part of Marjorie's 'tip' is correct. Cut the food into a smaller portion. Half is good, a third is better, a quarter is best! Instead of focusing on the whole portion, just focus on the reduced one as though that were the entirety. So let's say you've gone and bought yourself a giant cookie because you saw it in the shop and got a craving for it. No problem at all. Just remember to break it into a smaller portion. Then eat that portion slowly and really savor it – I mean REALLY savor it! Preferably eat it just after you've had a meal so you're not starving hungry and tempted to wolf down the whole thing. Definitely have a drink on the side. The point is, you can ENJOY this food, or at least this portion of it, so that you satisfy your craving. The remainder? You can either store this for another day or simply throw it away. You don't need the whole thing, you really don't – you can get just as much enjoyment from a small portion!

Same goes for a meal that's supercalorific (as Mary Poppins might have said). A big, tasty piece of lasagne, oozing and bubbling with cheese – delicious, right? My mouth's watering just thinking about it! But at the same time, you and I know that this meal is going to contain an awful lot of those wretched calories that we're trying to cut down on. But don't deny yourself the lasagne if it's what you really want. Have it. Enjoy it. But REDUCE it first. Use Marjorie's tip – cut it in half (or a third, or a quarter), and put the remainder out of sight for now. Just focus on enjoying the smaller portion that's in front of you. With something like lasagne or pizza, you can even scrape off some of the extra cheese to make the portion even less calorific (because let's face it, sometimes there is WAY too much cheese!), and just focus on enjoying the remaining ingredients with a much more appropriate smattering of cheese. Your brain recognizes that you are eating one of your favorite foods and still responds in the usual way, releasing those happy, feel-good hormones. Your tastebuds still get the delicious sensation of the sweet / savoury taste you've chosen to enjoy. Your stomach still gets to be pleasantly filled. And YOU get to eat your favorite foods with only a fraction of the calories and a fraction of the guilt!

As well as the food you eat, remember to ENJOY the overall experience of your weight loss journey. Regularly give yourself compliments on how well you're doing. As you see your weight starting to reduce, you'll be filled with a natural sense of pride and accomplishment. Really relish this; it's proof that you have put your mind towards something and are sticking with it.

I honestly feel excited about food now, but in a totally different way. Whereas previously I used to be excited about what tasty snack or meal I was going to gorge on next, now I think about how much I'm going to enjoy the food that I choose to eat within my (loose) calorie guidelines. I can't wait until next weigh-in day, when I'm almost certain that my weight will be where I want it to be. I love and enjoy receiving compliments from people who haven't seen me in a while and say 'gosh you're looking well, have you lost weight?'. This is far more enjoyable to me than a big greasy pizza, or family sized bag of potato chips – and the enjoyment lasts a lot longer than the momentary pleasure of those unhealthy foods!

NEXT STEPS

OK, so you've followed the chapters in this short book. You've managed to lose weight, and have now reached your target weight. CONGRATULATIONS! So now you can go back to eating what you whatever you want, whenever you want, right? Well, not really, unfortunately!

Once you have achieved your ideal weight, you can certainly cut yourself some slack, and no longer be as rigid with your calorie counting (not that the method in this book requires you to be particularly rigid in the first place!). Obviously once you've reached your target weight you don't want to carry on losing weight, as otherwise you'll be in danger of becoming underweight. So you can start using a process of trial and error to ensure that you remain at the correct weight.

Remember that the recommended daily calorie count for women is 2,000, and for men it's 2,500. So I believe that so long as you keep your daily calorie levels at or below these figures, you shouldn't be putting on weight. You now have power over your weight, rather than the other way around; you can choose to make it stay the same, go down, or even go up if necessary, just by remembering a few numbers, sticking to some very simple rules, and making minor adjustments to your eating habits which should in no way diminish your enjoyment of food.

What you've actually done using the techniques in this book is start an amazing process, one which has completely changed your mindset around what you put in your body. You've proved to yourself that you have the willpower to put subtle yet powerful changes into practice, changes which will lead to a healthier, slimmer you. And using the techniques in this book you'll have learned how to create a balance between eating whatever you want, and avoiding those excess calories which inevitably lead to weight gain. You've done the hard part. All you now need to do is maintain your new, healthy habits.

The best way of doing this is simply to keep an eye on your weight. Every few days, hop onto the scales to see how you're doing. If your weight remains stable, you know that you're doing exactly what you need to be doing, and that you're on the right track. So just carry on carrying on! However, once you have lost weight it's very easy to slip back into your old bad habits. You'll probably tell yourself, 'well, seeing as I went to all that effort to lose that weight there's no harm in me eating whatever I want now - I deserve it!', or 'well, I lost the weight so easily last time, if I put weight on again I'll just follow the same process to lose it all again'.

Both of the statements are understandable, and perhaps even justified to a degree. But ask yourself: do I really want to get into a situation where my weight is constantly fluctuating? Where I switch between careful, mindful eating, and wild abandon? If so, then that's your decision. But personally, I have found that a consistent, conscious approach is much more effective. This way you can keep your weight in line with where it should be, and just make small adjustments as necessary.

Since losing my weight I have found myself regularly going out for afternoon cake, or having dessert whenever I want. But I'm always aware in the back of my mind that this could quickly get out of control, leading me back into my old habits. So I simply weigh myself every few days. If I find that my weight has increased by a couple of pounds, I know that I'm probably consuming more calories than my body can cope with, and I'll cut back on some of the cake or dessert (often I'll still have it, but I'll consciously choose to only eat half a slice / portion, and leave the rest, as explained in Chapter 5). Or I'll remind myself that even though the meal I'm eating is delicious, this doesn't mean I have to clear my plate! In fact, it's quite a useful trick to get into the habit of always ensuring there's something left on your plate at the end of each meal.

Just making mental notes to yourself as you're eating helps reinforce your conscious awareness about your commitment to eating healthily. This in turn will filter through into your subconscious, and you'll find yourself making the right choices about calorie intake without even thinking about it. So continue to monitor your weight, and if it's going the wrong way, make the necessary minor adjustments until you see the figure on the scales coming back down to where it should be. Remember that as you age your metabolism changes, so the number of calories you can comfortably consume without gaining weight is likely to be considerably different at age 50 than it was at age 25. This is why it's so important to continue with the monitoring of your weight; you need to keep in line with the aging process, to keep making those minor adjustments to what you eat to ensure that body and mind are aligned.

This proactive weight monitoring process, together with your conscious (and subsequently unconscious) calorie control decisions is a winning combination, and one that should enable you to get to, and remain at, the weight you want to be, for the rest of your life! These are the steps I followed, and continue to follow, to address the concerns that I was having with my weight after years of eating mindlessly. I'm amazed when I look back at how unhealthily I used to eat, and kind of surprized that it took so long to catch up with me! But as sure as night follows day, an unhealthy diet will eventually lead to weight gain, and possibly a host of other problems too. I find it amazing how a little bit of mental discipline has led to such a significant change; not only do I look healthier, I feel healthier too! I can once again wear the clothes that I left hanging in my wardrobe for all those years, hoping I'd fit into them one day. People comment on my weight loss, telling me how well it suits me, and asking me what my secret is. Well, it's not a secret any more, because I've set out my entire strategy here. I truly believe this has been an incredibly effective yet simple solution to losing my excess weight, without sacrificing any of the foods I love or having to spend hours & hours exercising away the calories in a sweaty gym. I really hope that it can work for you too.

Good luck, and happy eating!

Did you enjoy this book? If so why not leave a review! Reviews help authors receive recognition and spread the word about their work:

https://www.amazon.com/review/create-review/?
ie=UTF8&channel=glance-detail&asin=1793119619

ABOUT THE AUTHOR

Anthony Williams is a successful business owner. He graduated in English Literature from the University of Warwick. After a career mostly spend in the insurance industry, he set up his own petsitting business with his partner in 2015. He lives in Birmingham, UK.

Disclaimer

All information and tools presented herein are intended for educational purposes. Any health, diet or exercise advice is not intended as medical diagnosis or treatment. You should always consult your doctor / physician or a qualified practitioner before embarking on a weight loss program.

The author disclaims all liability or loss in conjunction with any content provided here.

Lightning Source UK Ltd.
Milton Keynes UK
UKHW041655251120
374024UK00022B/131

9 781793 119612